MAGIC MUSHROOM CULTIVATION

THE ESSENTIAL GUIDE TO PSILOCYBIN GROW KIT

DENNIS CARTWELL

CHAPTER ONE

INTRODUCTION TO

MUSHROOMS

Psilocybin mushrooms, also known as shrooms or magic mushrooms, are polyphyletic, or informal group of fungi that contain psilocin and has hallucinating effects. These mushrooms have been be used in indigenous New World cultures in religious, divinatory, or spiritual contexts. Psilocybin mushrooms may be depicted in Stone Age rock art in Europe and Africa, but they are famously represented in the Pre-Columbian sculptures and glyphs that are present throughout Central and South America.

Prehistoric rock art in Spain, gives a hypothesis that Psilocybin mushroom was used in religious rituals 6,000 years ago. The Psilocybe genus species with hallucinogenic effects have been named among the native

4

peoples of Mesoamerica for divination, religious communion, and healing, from pre-Columbian times to modern day. In Guatemala were found mushroom stones and motifs. While in west Mexican state of Colima were found a statuette dating from ca. 200 CE. Suggesting mushroom strongly resembling Psilocybe mexicana in a shaft and chamber tomb.

To the Aztecs, a Psilocybe species known as teōnanācatl (which literally means "divine mushroom") was reportedly served at the coronation of the Aztec ruler Moctezuma II in 1502. The Mazatecs and Aztecs referred to psilocybin mushrooms as divinatory mushrooms, wondrous mushrooms, and genius mushrooms, when translated into English. It was Bernardino de Sahagún who reported the ritualistic use of *teonanácatl* by the Aztecs when he traveled to Central America after the expedition of Hernán Cortés.

The Catholic missionaries after the Spanish conquest, campaigned against the cultural tradition of the Aztecs, dismissing the use of hallucinogenic plants and mushrooms of the Aztecs as idolatry and together with other pre-Christian traditions, it was quickly suppressed. It was believed that such hallucinogenic plants and mushrooms, allowed the Aztecs and others to communicate with devils. Despite this, the use of *teonanácatl* persisted in some remote areas.

In modern time, the first mention of hallucinogenic mushrooms in any medicinal literature was in 1799's London Medical and Physical Journal: where a man served *Psilocybe semilanceata* mushrooms he had picked for breakfast to his family in London's Green Park. The doctor who treated the family, described how the youngest child "was attacked with fits of immoderate laughter, nor could the threats of his father or mother refrain him."

Gordon Wasson and Valentina Pavlovna Wasson in 1955, became the first known European Americans to participate actively in an indigenous mushroom ceremony. The Wassons publicized their experience by going as far as publishing an article on May 13, 1957. Roger Heim in 1956 identified the psychoactive mushroom that brought back by the Wassons from Mexico as *Psilocybe*, and Albert Hofmann was the first identify psilocybin and psilocin as the active compounds found in *Psilocybe* mushrooms in 1958.

Timothy Leary being inspired by the Wassons' *Life* article, he traveled down to Mexico to experience psilocybin mushrooms for himself. At his return to Harvard in 1960, Timothy Leary and Richard Alpert began the Harvard Psilocybin Project, this promoted the psychological and religious study of psilocybin and other psychedelic drugs. In 1963, Leary and Alpert were both dismissed by Harvard and they turned their attention towards the promotion of the psychedelic experience to the nascent hippie counterculture.

The activities of Wasson, Leary, Robert Anton Wilson, Terence McKenna and several others led to an explosion in the use of psilocybin mushrooms all across the globe.

In the early years of 1970s, many psilocybin mushroom species were widely identified from temperate North America, Asia, and Europe. Several articles were later published, describing methods of cultivating large quantities *of Psilocybe cubensis*. With the availability of psilocybin mushrooms from wild and other cultivated sources, they have become one of the most widely used psychedelic drugs.

CHAPTER TWO

TYPES OF PSILOCYBIN MUSHROOM

There are several poisonous mushrooms that looks very much like the 'magic mushrooms' and it has sometimes been difficult for pickers to differentiate them. Misidentification of psilocybin mushrooms and the consumption of poisonous mushroom has resulted in several illness and in some cases even death across the globe.

Psilocybin mushrooms might just be the "next best thing" in holistic healing and wellness. Also known as "magic mushrooms", there exist over 200 varieties of mushrooms with psychoactive properties. Psilocybin mushrooms are so incredible and mysterious, ranging from the beautiful experiences they occasion to the mystical compounds that they naturally produce. Some species have dozens of different strains with their own signature shape, flavor, and trip However, for the purpose of study, we shall be mentioning just a handful of the most common and widespread psilocybin mushrooms.

Psilocybe cubensis

Psilocybe cubensis are one of the easiest mushroom to cultivate indoors, and from time immemorial, there have been very few important books teaching hobby growers how to grow and care for them. While there

are several strains of cubensis are found in the wild all across the globe, the most potent of the strains are the indoor-grown cubensis. With several years of selective indoor-growing, there are currently about 60 different strains of Psilocybe cubensis. And in most cases, mushrooms bought in the underground market are often more effective than the ones that are picked in nature or wild. This is because when mushrooms are grown in specific substrates, it helps to increase their potency. Psilocybe cubensis are the easiest set of magic mushroom to cultivate indoors. And if you have consumed any psilocybin mushrooms, without knowing which specific species it was, there are chances that it was a strain of Psilocybe cubensis.

Psilocybe semilanceata (Liberty Caps)

According to Psilopedia, Liberty Caps are considered the most widespread naturally growing psilocybin mushroom in the world.

Also, but they are the third most potent mushrooms in the world, this is according to the tests done by a German chemist and mycologist, Paul Stamets and Jochen Gartz in 1997. Also known as Witch's Hats, they are found in the wild of the Northern Hemisphere and flourish well in rich and acidic soil, like meadows, grasslands, pastures, and lawns, most especially those fertilized with sheep or cow manure.

Even though Psilocybe semilanceata are found all over the world, it is extremely difficult to cultivate them indoors. While most Liberty Caps consumed around the world are picked in the wild, caution is required when identifying them because they can easily be confused with other similar looking poisonous species that grow in the same region. Liberty Caps have a conical or bell-shaped cap, where the name is derived from, and they reportedly taste similar to flour.

Psilocybe cyanescens

This specie of mushroom are also known as the 'Wavy Cap' because of the rippled nature

of its cap. Wavy Cap are believed to be native to Central Europe and the Pacific Northwest and was first formally identified by Elsie Wakefield in England in 1946, even though Psilopedia reported that she had been collecting Cyans since 1910. Psilocybe cyanescens loves woody debris, like the wood chips and mulch that populate gardens, trails, and parks.

While these variety of mushrooms are tough to grow indoors, they are popular among mushroom identifiers because of their strength. According to Stamets, psilocybe cyanescens are known to be potent and can contain between 0.3 percent to 1.68 percent psilocybin, 0.28 percent to 0.51 percent psilocin, and 0.02 percent to 0.03 percent baeocystin. Although Wavy Cap still produce substantial effects when dried but are stronger when eaten fresh.

Psilocybe Cyanofibrillosa:

This is a small wood-loving Psilocybe common to the Pacific coast of the United States of America, from San Francisco to British Columbia. They are not considered to  be particularly potent, containing only around 0.25% alkaloids by dried weight. However, there are proves to suggest that a greater percentage of alkaloids are lost on drying this variety than with other species, therefore making fresh Psilocybe cyanofibrillosa specimens more potent than they are expected to be.

Psilocybe Bohemica

This is a central European relative of the North American lignicolous Psilocybes, found in Austria, Germany, and the Czech Republic. They are similar to the Psilocybes azurescens and Psilocybes cyanofibrillosa in appearance and are slightly less potent than

Psilocybes cyanescens, averaging around 1.1

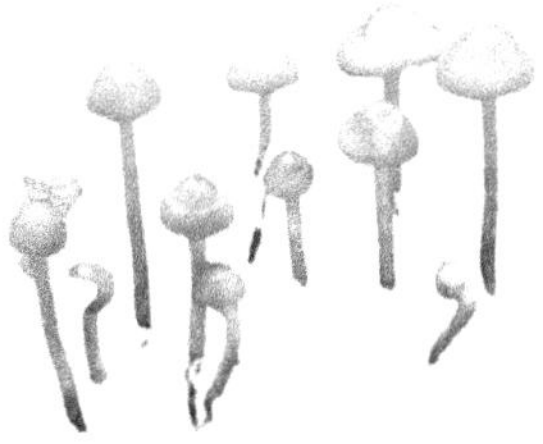

% alkaloids by dried weight.

PEST AND DISEASES OF MUSHROOM

Mushroom Fly

These are pest capable of causing bodily harm to our grown mushrooms. They are tiny and dark coloured creatures with a very short lifespan and thrive off of mycelium and compost. They measure between 2-8 millimeters in length and sometimes act as pollinators for mushroom spores. Mushroom flies are known to be weak flyers and they often choose to walk over plants and soil and originate from various different families, among which are Sciaridae, Mycetophilidae, Ditomyiidae, Bolitophilidae, Keroplatidae, and Diadocidiidae.

They are hardy creatures and are capable of surviving very cold temperatures and a female mushrooms fly can lay between 50 to 300 eggs into compost and through transformation process develop into an adult fly.

Several problems may arise if your mushroom kit has been hit by a mushroom fly infestation. Both the adult mushroom flies and their larva feast on the compost that your mushrooms gets its nourishment from as well as the mycelium networks underneath them. By so doing, these mushroom flies may compromise best yields.

HOW TO PREVENT MUSHROOM FLIES

It is preferably much better for mushroom growers to carry out preventative measures in order to avoid an infestation from taking place. To prevent this from taking place, tobacco and coffee grounds can be introduced into the growing kit in order to deter these pests.

The most efficient and effective way of preventing the presence of mushroom flies is probably by pasteurizing your choice of substrate. By so doing, it will ensure that any pests already present in your substrate will be eliminated even before you start cultivating your mushrooms. To do this, you have to preheat your oven to 93 degree Celsius. Get a baking tray and fill in some of your compost and use a thermometer to monitor the temperature of the middle of the soil. Once the middle of your material reaches 71 degrees Celsius, allow it bake for 30 minutes.

HOW TO FIGHT MUSHROOMS

FLIES

Once it is realized that your mushrooms are being attack by mushroom flies, there are different methods that can be use in order to ensure that you successfully them and to avoid any potential damage to your mushrooms. These flies can be defeated using chemicals as an option, also, there are natural and organic options to deter them.

With the resources and space, one of the natural options would be the introduction of some new pets into your home, in the form of natural predators. Example is the Venus fly traps, which might be a good option for some. This will settle into the humid climate of your grow space and will munch away a reasonable number of the invading species.

You can also introduce praying mantis into your magic mushroom growing space to take out the threat in their highly accurate and stealthy ways. Praying mantis can grow quite large and impractical, but however, whilst they are still young, they can serve as great bodyguards for your mushroom grow.

Similarly, predatory mites can also be used to control mushroom fly larvae. At their larval stage, predatory nematodes also attack other insects including mushroom flies.

On my final note on natural predators that could help to prevent and tackle the potential problem of mushroom flies is parasitic wasps.

CHAPTER THREE

HEALTH BENEFITS OF MAGIC MUSHROOMS

<u>Mushrooms fight cancer</u>

A research documented in the Journal of Experimental Biology and Medicine shows that all the common varieties of mushroom reduced breast cancer cells by a whopping 33 percent. This however are not the only type of cancer mushrooms help. Another studies on prostate and stomach cancer show similar results.

<u>Boost immune and high in vitamins</u>

In mushrooms are found beta-glucan and lentinan,+ two properties that give your immune system a much-needed boost and are high in crucial vitamins such as vitamin D, and B12, which makes them an excellent choice for vegetarians since B12 is most common in animal products.

Lowers Depression

Researches has proven that psilocybin mushrooms are effective at treating depression very well, as well as treating post-traumatic stress disorder. Lately, a prestigious study group in London have undertaken a study that suggests psilocybin could be used to treat major depression. Twelve patients were given 2 doses of psilocybin, one low and one high, and also combined with psychological support. Just a week after the 2nd dose, depression scores were significantly reduced in almost all patients, with 8/12 of the patients showing no sign of depression. After three months, it was recorded that five of the patients were still depression- free, and four out of the remaining seven patients had a reduction in the rating of their depression from "Severe" to "Mild or Moderate".

Stimulates Growth of New Brain Cells

A research carried out by the University of South Florida and published in 2013 studied the effects of magic mushrooms on fear-conditioned mice. What they found surprised them. The main build-up of magic mushrooms, psilocybin, helped the mice to get over their fear and promoted new neurons growth and regeneration in their brains.

The research leader, Dr. Briony Catlow of the Lieber Institute for Brain Development had a few things to say after this research: "Memory, learning, and the ability to relearn that a once threatening stimuli is no longer a danger absolutely depends on the ability of the brain to alter its connections. We believe that neuroplasticity plays a critical role in psilocybin accelerating fear extinction. It is highly possible that in the future we will continue these studies since many interesting questions have come up from these experiments. The hope is that we can extend the findings to humans in clinical trials."

<u>Helps In The Treatment Of Cluster Headaches</u>

Cluster headaches are most times described as the most disruptive and painful type of headache to experience. This cluster headaches are more intense than the migraine headaches, but they typically don't last as long. Although the effects at night are often more painful and intense than during the daytime cluster headache attacks, but the two obviously interfere in a person's life significantly.

Till this moment, no systematic research have been published that describe the treatment potential of psilocybin for headaches, but thousands of anecdotal reports have been brought to the attention of the medical community. In the middle of 2000s, medical professionals started taking notice of psilocybin and LSD as possible treatments for cluster headaches after some of their patients reported remission of their condition following self-medication and recreational psychedelic use.

A recent study has reported that psilocybin could be a more effective treatment of cluster headaches more than any of the currently available medications, with nearly 50% of sufferers reporting psilocybin as a completely effective treatment.

<u>Alleviates Obsessive-Compulsive Disorder Symptoms</u>

Obsessive-compulsive disorder is a psychiatric disorder which occurs most especially in patients suffering from schizophrenia, bipolar disorders and other form of psychiatric ailments. A research carried out by the University of Arizona in 2006 found out that magic mushrooms are very effective in mitigate the symptoms of this disorder.

MUSHROOM POISONING AND SAFETY CONCERNS

Mushroom toxicity or mushroom poisoning usually occurs when there is the ingestion of mushrooms that contain toxins, which are in most cases in the context of foraging for nontoxic and are similarly appearing as nontoxic mushrooms. Several species of mushrooms causes toxicity when ingested and their symptoms vary from species to species. Mushrooms have evolved side by side with plants for millions of years, they are higher fungi fruiting bodies and are widely distributed all around the world. Thousands of mushrooms species exist, but only about 100 mushrooms species cause symptoms when they are eaten by humans, and of the 100, only 15-20 species of mushroom are potentially lethal when ingested.

It is very difficult when differentiating between toxic and nontoxic mushroom species in the wild, even for those that are knowledgeable about mushrooms. There are no simple rule when distinguishing the edible mushrooms from toxic mushrooms. The same species of mushroom may have varying degrees of toxicity depending on the location and when the mushroom was harvested.

Research has shown that more than 95% of mushroom poisoning cases occurs when there is misidentification of the mushroom species by a novice mushroom hunter and less than 5% cases of mushroom poisoning occurs when such mushrooms are consumed for its mind-altering properties. The degree of mushroom poisoning may be different depending on the location such mushroom was grown, the growth conditions, the level of toxin present in the mushroom and the genetic characteristics of such mushrooms. In some mushrooms, freezing, cooking, boiling or even processing them may not alter the toxicity content of such mushroom. When a patients have consumed an unidentified mushroom, when such species is identified, it will help to determine the specific treatment to be administered.

The differences in clinical effects may vary depending on an individual's susceptibility and on the presence of other confounding factors such as contamination or co-ingestion. Given to the fact that an experienced mycologist are in most cases not readily available for immediate consultation and treatment when a patients become ill after mushroom ingestion, such treatment is usually guided by the visible symptoms.

Every poisonous species of mushroom contains 1 or more toxins that can be classified on the basis of it's physiologic and clinical effects in humans. The clinical spectrum and toxicity depends on the following factors:

> Individual response to the toxins
> The species consumed
> The location the mushroom is grown
> The amount consumed
> The method of preparation

Never consume any wild mushroom without first obtaining an expert opinion of identification of such mushrooms.

HOW LONG DOES PSILOCYBIN LAST?

The average time that a psilocin effects is felt in the body before it is eliminated is 50 minutes. Generally, the rate at which it take for a substance to be entirely eliminated from the system varies on individuals. Psilocin as the case may be, is usually eliminated from the body through the kidneys in the urine in about three hours. The metabolism of psilocybin mushrooms differs in people, as it is faster in some persons than others. Dosage is a major factor to consider when looking at how long a psilocybin stays in the body, also is the frequency of use, as well as age, and weight. What is experienced by psilocybin consumers is highly determined by their mindset and the physical setting, and these put together is often referenced as "set and setting."

In a 2017 study of healthy adults, it was discovered that the psilocin levels peak after about 80 minutes, corresponding with the average peak in effects after 90 minutes, but this varies across individuals. The instantaneous effects of using psilocybin mushrooms wear off in about 6 to 12 hours, although most people report the continues feeling of the effects until they sleep and a "glow" the next day.

Urine

Psilocybin was not included in the standard five- and nine-panel drug tests ordered by most drug testing companies, but companies such as NMS Labs and Quest Diagnostics do offer urine tests for psilocybin and psilocin, one of its metabolites that could be purchased by probation office or an employer. After 24 hours of ingestion, only small traces of the drug are detectable by a urine test.

Blood

Blood testing for psilocybin mushroom is not common, although it may be permitted under some certain conditions. The detection period is however very brief, which means that the test must be administered within hours after use.

Hair

Magic mushrooms like many other substances, can be found in hair follicles for period of 90 days. Tests such as these may however require larger hair samples in order to find detectable amounts of the substance.

FACTORS THAT AFFECT

DETECTION TIME

The time that is required for the body to excrete psilocybin depends on many variables. It can sometimes be very tricky determining how long "magic mushrooms" stay in the system. The mushroom species has a great influence on the detection times. The specific psilocybin mushroom that is consumed affects how quickly the metabolite is eliminated from the human body. Magic mushroom has more than 100 species and each of them have varying levels of psilocybin content, ranging from psilocybe azurenscens with 1.78% to psilocybe tampanensis with 0.68% to psilocybe liniformans with 0.16%.

The frequency at which psilocybin is eliminated from the body depends on the dosage, how frequent it was use, the specie of mushroom, the body metabolism, and other factors include how much you weigh, your age, the body hydration level, and the health of your body systems.

A look at some factors that can affect psilocybin metabolism include:

Body Weight: research has found that people with higher body mass tend to excrete psilocybin faster than those with low BMIs, your body mass therefore is crucial in determining the longevity of magic mushroom in your system.

Age: this also determine how long psilocybin will last in the system as people who are over the age 65 tend to have reduced blood flow to their kidneys and liver, these can delay the excretion of psilocybin from the system.

The Activity Levels: The more physically active that people are, the faster they excrete psilocybin because their metabolism rates is higher.

Hydration Levels: The excretion of psilocybin can be speed up by water in the system.

Liver And Kidney Function: Those with liver or kidney disease could experience more difficulty in the time it takes for psilocybin to pass through the system.

Injection Vs Ingestion: The intravenously injected magic mushroom is much faster to excrete than those that is consumed by oral ingestion. It takes about 7 to 8 hours for psilocybin to be cleared from the body when injected.

SYMPTOMS OF OVERDOSE

You need caution whenever handling mushrooms that are from the wild. It is important that you get an expert to observe all the mushrooms that you pick yourself before eating them to ensure proper identification. Sometimes, even an experienced mushroom hunters can misidentify a highly poisonous mushroom for the one they intended to gather. The side effects of mushroom poisoning can be catastrophic and result in liver damage and death except when there is an immediate access to a liver transplant. Don't wait to experience symptoms, it is better you call 911 when there is suspected case of mushroom poisoning, or call poison control right away at 800-222-122.

The physical overdose on species of magic mushrooms that are correctly identified is not likely, in other cases, some people do have what is known as "bad trip," in which they experience loss of awareness, confusion, and exposure to challenging psychological material.

A bad trip is an indicator of a need for more in-depth psychological support and largely a product of "set" and "setting". Study has shown that bad or difficult trips are minimized when we attend to the basic physical needs before and during the experience, checking in with a trusted friend, keeping overstimulation to a minimum, and using lower doses.

If you are someone with a trauma disorder or other ongoing psychological condition, it is important that you talk to a psychologist before taking psilocybin. Psychedelic experiences may bring psychological material into your awareness which you may find challenging, and it is also helpful to be aware of that in advance and have a plan for working it out.

HOW TO STOP A BAD TRIP

Even though it is very difficult or impossible to "switch off" the effects gotten from drugs that are hallucinogenic in nature, a bad trip can however be transformed into a more positive experience when the people having the trip is open to being comforted or supported. In most cases, listening to soothing music and lying down in the presence of a calm support person can help. The most crucial time of the trip typically occurs from 1 hour to 3 hours after the drug is consumed, the most intense aspects of the trip usually get eased with time, however the effects often continue for the next 6 to 12 hours after that, at this period of time the person will not be able to sleep.

If the people experiencing bad trip are open to receiving medical help, what they view as intensely unpleasant aspects of the trip could be alleviated, they could be accompanied to a walk-in clinic or the emergency room. There exist several medical interventions that could be of help. Never try self-medication by taking other drugs, this is highly risky and could worsen the effects of the trip or could even cause drug interactions.

Not taking hallucinogenic drugs is the best way to avoid a bad trip. While you may be intrigued by the idea of tripping, there is a reason that people don't usually take them for long—sooner or later, they usually have a bad trip, and never want to repeat the experience. So my best advice is to ignore peer pressure, don't take psychedelic drugs, and that way, they won't give you a bad trip. Hallucinogens can be extracts from plants and mushrooms or can be man-made. A large doses of psilocybin can produce effects that is similar to the powerful hallucinogen LSD. "Magic mushrooms" as sometimes called can be used either fresh or dried. Magic mushrooms are normally eaten, brewed like tea for drinking or mixed with food.

CHAPTER FOUR

THE LEGALITY OF MAGIC MUSHROOMS

The legality of psilocybin mushrooms varies from country to country across the globe. Under the United Nations 1971 Convention on Psychotropic Substances, Psilocybin and psilocin are among drugs listed as Schedule I drugs and as such, magic mushrooms are also illegal to possess, grow, sell or purchase in several countries of the world. It is however important to say that some countries have interpreted the Vienna Convention to connote psilocybin mushrooms are not as illegal as psilocybin itself, and have created exceptions to the cultivation, use or sell.

WHERE ARE MAGIC MUSHROOMS LEGAL?

Although psilocybin mushrooms are illegal in the **Netherlands**, there is a loophole in the law that allows for the growth, purchase, and use of "magic truffles." Truffles has the same stage of development of a mushroom, and truffles of psilocybin mushroom species still possess large quantities of psilocybin.

It is legal to possess, grow, consume, and purchase magic mushrooms in **Brazil**, although the substance itself (psilocybin) is technically illegal. In Brazilian law, there are specific laws that have been written about illegal activities and none of these laws are related to possession of fresh mushroom for consumption or sale.

In **British Virgin Islands**, it is prohibited to transport and sale magic mushrooms, but possession and personal use is however legal. Vendors may even sell them to tourists and there will not be any apparent consequences.

In **Jamaica,** there seem to be no problem with the use of magic mushroom, and in the country, there are even a number of mushroom retreats.

The possession, consumption of psilocybin mushrooms in **Austria** is decriminalized, but if you are found with them, you may be required to attend therapy. It is also permitted for you to grow your own mushrooms, so long as you don't ingest them and they are for aesthetic purposes.

There is restrictions on psilocybin mushrooms in **Canada**, but it is legally for to purchase mushroom spores. The growth of magic mushrooms for ingestion could be interpreted as manufacture of a prohibited substance under Canadian law, I will strongly advise against it cultivation in Canada.

In **Czech Republic,** the cultivation of psilocybin mushrooms has been decriminalized so long that you are growing only a "small" quantity. The possession of large quantity of magic mushroom is still illegal.

In **Mexico**, it is officially illegal to possess, grow and sell Psilocybin mushrooms, but however, the authorities turn a blind eye to traditional or sacramental use and cultivation of fresh magic mushrooms, in the Vienna Convention, there is an exception for sacramental use of plant medicines.

In **Portugal**, you can possess small amounts of magic mushrooms without going to jail as it has been decriminalized. But however, when you get caught, you will end up going to court-mandated rehabilitation or therapy.

Personal use of psilocybin mushrooms in **Spain** has been decriminalized. However, there is ambiguity surrounding the use of spores and grow kits and the legality of having small amounts of fresh mushrooms. Further research on the legality of magic mushroom in Spain is advised.

There are some big exceptions to the prohibition of magic mushrooms in the **United States**. It is surprisingly legal to buy psilocybin mushroom spores in some states so long that you are not going to use them to grow mushrooms. However in some states, it is prohibited to sell spores, such states include Georgia, Idaho and California. Magic mushrooms have been **decriminalized in Oakland** and **Denver**. This is an example that other US cities may follow this example and make their own specific psilocybin mushroom laws.

MAGIC MUSHROOMS MOLECULE

Scientific research have shown how magic mushrooms make the molecules that is behind its trippy hallucinatory effects. This discovery could help in mass production of compounds which the doctors have termed to be useful for treatment of wide range of mental disorders.

The active ingredient in magic mushrooms is a compound called psilocybin, it was chemist Albert Hoffman that first described these in 1958. When consumed, the body converts it to the molecule psilocin, that interacts with brain receptors to produce the hallucinations and euphoria magic mushrooms are known with.

Magic mushrooms have attracted interest from psychologists and other doctors of the medical field, who have discovered that psilocybin may be useful in treating depression, anxiety, post-traumatic stress disorder (PTSD) and other brain related illnesses. These effects explain the drug's long popularity.

A small amount of magic mushrooms in the genus Psilocybe produced a reasonable amounts of the psychoactive molecule, pharmacist and chemists have discovered a few ways of making psilocybin in the lab. But until now, there was no scientific research that was able to explain how the mushrooms did it, or if their techniques could harness to make the compound by ourselves. There is now a change, thanks to research reported in Angewandte Chemie [a weekly scientific journal].

Dirk Hoffmeister a Microbiologist recreated in a test tube the natural process that magic mushrooms use in making psilocybin. He identified four major enzymes that convert the starting material, 4-hydroxyl-Ltryptophan, into the psychoactive final product. (In our bodies is tryptophan which is a nutrient molecule used as a starting point in order to make a number of naturally important compounds, which includes neurochemicals like melatonin and serotonin.)

The method used by Hoffmeister and his team only took five steps, starting with a molecule with two joined rings, moving through a series of careful additions and removals of different chemical motifs, and by ending with the closure of third ring joined to the first two. His team identified a new group of enzymes, psilocybin decarboxylases, which was discovered after sequencing two magic mushrooms' genomes. The new group of enzymes are key to kicking off the natural process that makes psilocybin.

Researchers have said that Hoffmeister's method could be the basis for pharmaceutical psilocybin production. His group genetically modified E. coli bacteria to enable the enzymes mushrooms use to generate psilocybin, this could have set precedence for pharmaceutical companies. Hoffmeister's work has also been applauded by Medicinal chemists. "The new work lays the foundation for developing a fermentation process for production of this powerful psychedelic fungal drug, which has a fascinating history and pharmacology," Courtney Aldrich of the University of Minnesota, Twin Cities, addressed Chemical & Engineering News.

THE THERAPY

Magic mushroom therapy refers to any type of professional use of psilocybin to treat depression and anxiety. The active ingredient found in "magic" mushrooms is psilocybin. Psilocybin therapy is not used in conventional medical practice because of the absence of medical evidence for efficacy and safety, and also for the legal concerns.

Over the years, studies on psilocybin therapy have depended on self-reports from patients. But in a more recent time, a study published in 2017 by a group of researchers who went deep to underscore the mechanisms behind psilocybin and how it affects patients with depression treatment-resistant.

They made use of MRI technology to scan cerebral blood flow and brain activity before and after psilocybin ingestion. All the patients following the treatment, saw a decrease in their depressive symptoms within one week, and the decrease experienced lasted for at least five weeks in nearly half of them. Joining these impressive results with the patient brain scans, they found a correlation between blood flow being reduced in the areas that handle emotional responses, stress, and fear. Although there is not enough research to support the efficacy of psilocybin therapy, but even the few studies that have taken on psilocybin therapy are all leading to a promising findings.

What can psilocybin therapy treat?

Several research into psilocybin therapy has only end up examining the depression and anxiety efficacy of psilocybin therapy, but it has also demonstrated to possess the potential of treating other mental disorders like PTSD, cluster headaches, and addiction.

When we carefully study the "reset" mechanism hypothesis of magic mushrooms, it is possible to get a clearer picture of how psilocybin therapy may work. By ingestion of psilocybin in a therapeutic setting, it can detach from our default state, which in most cases is corrupted or oppressive. Psilocybin therapy unlike many existing treatments, occurs in a single session or series of sessions, and there may not be need to continue use because a single powerful experience of psilocybin therapy can deliver a lasting results. Psilocybin therapy may be useful as an occasional refresh for general wellbeing of the body, even for those without depression, anxiety, or other treatment resistant mental disorders.

Can I try psilocybin therapy on my own?

Trying psilocybin therapy on your own is not a bad idea, but however, there are several things that you must consider before doing so and the things to consider are; the legality of magic mushroom in your country, efficacy, and safety.

When doing this on your own, it is highly advised that you find someone to help facilitate your experience and keep you safe. It is not advisable to use psilocybin alone, especially when it comes to you attempting to treat some mental disorder, this can result in distress and even endanger your health when you are not properly prepared.

While the ultimate goal is to allow psilocybin do the work, it will be most effective when set up and facilitated by experienced people. It may be difficult to get the result of a dedicated psilocybin retreat center on your own. These psilocybin therapeutic centers usually employ several staff members and experts who are all well trained to manage the therapeutic potential of your psilocybin experience.

CHAPTER FIVE

THE SPIRITUALITY OF

MAGIC MUSHROOM

There is really a spiritual effect of Magic mushrooms on people, according to the most rigorous look yet at this aspect of the fungus's active ingredient. It is relatively easy for those who have never consumed magic mushroom to argue that the visions and insights as experienced by users are mere "hallucinations." On the other hand, it is quite the opposite for the user. Users of psilocybin mushroom has often described the experiences they had on higher doses to be of such profundity that they are frequently described as something that can't be explained or described.

Psilocybin as an active ingredients of magic mushroom is a boundary dissolving compound which in some cases, strips the user of their sense of individuality and ego. Psilocybin user soon comes to realize and sense a deep interconnectedness with the other lifeforms of the world once their ego and contrived perceptions of one's place and purpose in the world is set aside. Often at times, this process is described in terms similar to a deeply spiritual or mystical experience. For psilocybin users, these experiences is thus far from a hallucination, and the sensations imparted and insights can often be seen as a turning point in one's life. Summarizing a typical psilocybin session, it can be argued that one of the major thing gained from these fungi is that all life has inherent value and to take care of that life.

The Good Friday or Marsh Chapel Experiment was one of the most famous scientific studies ever conducted with magic mushrooms. It was carried out in 1962 by Harvard graduate student Walter Pahnke under the supervisions and direction of Timothy Leary, this experimental research proved that psilocybin was able to reliably induce a mystical experience in a majority of the people who consume it, with several participants claiming it was amongst the top five most meaningful experiences in their lives.

In another study carried out by Rick Doblin of MAPS in 1991 and that of Roland Griffiths of Johns Hopkins University in 2006, showed similar results, about one-third of volunteers after taking psilocybin, in the carefully controlled research had a "complete" mystical experience with half of them explaining their encounter as the single most spiritually significant experience of their life. "Psilocybin is an amazing tool for unlocking the mysteries of human consciousness. The core feature of this mystical experience is a strong sense of inter-connectedness to all things, a rising sense of self-confidence, clarity and communal responsibility, altruism and social justice. Understanding the nature of these effects and their consequences, may very well be the key to survival of the human species." Given that magic mushrooms can produce mystical experiences is a major revelation in and of itself, but researchers have not stopped there and have however taken further step to see how this experience could be useful to humans in great need of a transformative awakening. A recent study from Imperial College London along these lines, found that psilocybin was also very effective at treatment of depression, with 12 out of 12 subjects experiencing major decrease in depression symptoms and 5 of 12 being completely healed of their depression 3 months later. In addition, psilocybin mushrooms have been used for the treatment of end-of-life anxiety in terminally ill cancer patients with similarly positive results.

RECREATIONAL USES OF MAGIC MUSHROOM

According to 2017 Global Drug Survey, Mushrooms are the safest of all the drugs people take recreationally. In 2016, more than 12,000 persons were reported have taken psilocybin hallucinogenic mushrooms and only 0.2% of them said they needed emergency medical treatment and the rate was at least five times lower than that for LSD, MDMA and cocaine.

Adam Winstock, a consultant addiction psychiatrist and founder of the Global Drug Survey, said "Magic mushrooms are one of the safest drugs in the world," pointed out that the only risk involved was people picking and eating the wrong mushrooms. "Death from toxicity is almost unheard of with poisoning with more dangerous fungi being a much greater risk in terms of serious harms."

The Global Drug Survey of 2017, which has almost 120,000 participants in 50 different countries, is so far the world's biggest yearly drug survey, the survey questions covers the types of substances people take, their patterns of use and if there be any negative effects experienced. A total of about 28,000 people were said to have taken magic mushrooms at some point in their lives, and about 81.7% seeking a "moderate psychedelic experience" and the "enhancement of environment and social interactions".

Winstock noted that psilocybin mushrooms are not completely harmless. "Combined use with alcohol and use within risky or unfamiliar settings increase the risks of harm most commonly accidental injury, panic and short lived confusion, disorientation and fears of losing one's mind." However, he advised people thinking of taking magic mushroom to plan "your trip carefully with trusted company in a safe place and always know what mushrooms you are using". In some cases people can experience panic attacks and flashbacks he added.

According to a separate piece of research carried out by Roland Griffiths and Robert Jesse at Johns Hopkins Medicine even bad trips can have positive outcomes. Their paper surveyed almost 2,000 individuals about their single most challenging experience or psychologically difficult with magic mushrooms. 2.7% of the group, received medical help and 7.6% of the group sought treatment for enduring psychological symptoms. However 84% of the people surveyed said they benefitted from the experience.

CHAPTER SIX

HOW DO MUSHROOMS

GROW?

Mushrooms are fungi that grows from spores and not seed. The spores are so tiny that they can't be seen individually with the naked eyes. Mushrooms are not plants but fruits of fungus called mycelium and does not necessarily depend on soil for their growth but rather, they rely on substances like straw, sawdust, grain or wood chips for nourishment.

Mushroom spawn are like the starter you will need to make sourdough bread. The spawn supports the growth of mycelium. The mycelium are the first part of the mushroom to grow and later transform into mushrooms. Mushrooms like cool, dark and humid environment and at home, the basement is an ideal location or also, a spot under the sink is perfect. The best temperature for mushrooms are between 55 and 60°F away from direct sunlight and heat. Mushrooms can tolerate some level of lights but are better off in a cool dark place with no disturbance.

WORKING WITH AGAR

Agar are polysaccharide that are derived from marine red algae. Their uniqueness is in their ability to remain liquid until cooling for as low as 36 degrees C or even below. A major advantage of working with agar is found in the ability of their nutrients and other growth media which can be mixed together before they get solidifies and they remain solid at room temperature. When you have mixed the solution together, you can then pour your mixture into the Petri dishes use for inoculating with one of the following items: a liquid culture, mushroom spores, live tissue from the mushroom itself or an agar wedge from a colonized Petri dish. It is important that you use live tissue in order to capture a desired species for cloning because of a unique characteristics that may be desired.

Types of media and their functionality.

> ➢ General Purpose Medium: This is a plan to grow a complete range of different microorganisms. Nutrient Agar is a general purpose media.
>
> ➢ Differential Medium: This can grow different types of microorganisms, and can be distinguished within them given to their different appearances on the medium; the color of the medium or color of the colonies where the organisms are growing.
>
> ➢ Enriched Medium: This media is endowed with some kind of unique growth factor such as serum, blood, hemoglobin and several others.
>
> ➢ Fermentation Medium: The Fermentation Medium shows whether a microorganism can ferment a given carbohydrate. This is an anaerobic process which often generates acids. Acid

is produced, when the carbohydrate is fermented, and this can be detected by a PH indicator dye.

> Selective Medium: just like the name 'selective medium', it contains a chemical that stops the growth of certain organisms while promoting the growth of others.

In growing magic mushrooms it is essential for you to use a Selective Medium, adding various minerals and nutrients. to promote the growth of the mycelium. You can even add antibiotics just to inhibit the growth of some certain bacteria.

There are several Agar recipes which can be used but the two most common are Malt Extract Agar (MEA) and Potato Dextrose Agar (PDA).

Malt Extract Agar (MEA)

9 grams agar agar

10 grams light malt extract

500 ml distilled or potable water

Potato Dextrose Agar (PDA)

500 ml distilled or potable water

Broth from boiling 150 grams sliced potatoes

7 grams dextrose

9 g agar agar

1 gram brewer yeast or yeast-extract (optional)

How to Use Agar Culture Medium.

While getting Agar recipes ready, you must understand that if there are too many nutrients added to your Agar, it becomes hypertonic. In essence, there will be a higher concentration of particles in the nutrient solution than those present in the dividing cells of your mycelium. It prefers balance. If your mycelium is placed into this hypertonic solution that you have, equilibrium will try to assert itself. This is given to the fact that the membranes of the mycelium are selectively permeable; which only permit certain things across the membrane. The water within the cell will move the membrane by osmosis to the outer part and the cells will dehydrate; inhibiting growth.

In preparing your Agar recipes, there will be the need for a container to sterilize your mixture in. A quart size jar will works perfectly for this. Bore a 3/8 inch hole in the metal lid of your container and fit the inside with a Tyvek filter disc. Mix your contents together thoroughly inside the quart jar. Secure your lid loosely on the jar and add into your pressure cooker (if like you can preheat your water to boiling point before adding your quart jar. This will help to prevent caramelization of your ingredients). Full your pressure cooker with water until it is approximately 1 in the water level is on the side of your jar. Sterilize your jar at 15 p.s.i for about 30-40 minutes.

When your sterilization time is over, allow your pressure cooker to cool to zero before open it. Open your pressure cooker in front of a flow-hood or your sterile glovebox can be used when pouring agar plates. Each of your recipe will fill above 20 agar plates.

Once your jar has cool down to touch and the contents is still liquefied, add in enough PDA or MEA to fill the bottom of your Petri dish. The more time spent to open the lids to air, the greater the chance for airborne contaminates to find their way into the culture medium. Leave your agar plates to cool to room temperature and solidify. If you like, you can choose to seal the edges with para-film just to help stave off bacteria contaminations.

Also, it is important that when inoculating agar plates, to use a sterile flowhood or glovebox to just to decrease their chances of contamination. Each of your agar plate can be inoculated with spores from a mature mushroom, agar wedges from a colonized plate, or a prepared liquid culture.

THE LIFE CYCLE OF PSILOCYBIN MUSHROOM

The life cycle of a mushroom is similar to the life cycle of filamentous Ascomycota in the formation monokaryons, there is a prolonged dikaryon stage before karyogamy. They spread when the veil on the underside of the cap opens. When the environment is right, the spores develop into mycelium. The mycelium is a living organism that may be compared to a plant. The fruiting body that ensures reproduction is what is known as mushroom and when the mushroom matures, they release their spores, mushroom complete their circle when they release their own spores.

The cultivation of mushroom are slightly risky, this because the developing mycelium is open to contamination. It is necessary that you sterilize your substrate beforehand, as well as inoculation in a clean and sterile environment. Within the space of two to four weeks (depending on the substrate size and temperature) your substrate will be fully colonized and will require for you to change environment. At the time of incubation, your mycelium should be kept in a warm and dark place. While fruiting, your mushroom does not only requires a protected environment, but also fresh air and light. In the space of two weeks your first mushrooms should be visible and they get matured in another seven days.

STEP BY STEP GUIDE TO CULTIVATING MUSHROOM

This is a simple guide that will lead you in the process of magic mushroom cultivation with spore syringe while using a Basic Growkit. This simple guide also works if you are using your own ingredients.

Ingredients:

220g rice flour

900 g vermiculite

4 paperclips

4 cultivation boxes (300ml) with air filter

Spore syringe

2 filter bags

Pair of sterile gloves

User manual

Mouth mask

Ingredients:

Pressure cooker

Nail or safety pin

Alcohol (or another disinfectant)

Spray bottle

Lighter or torch

Aluminium foil

Tape

Step 1 substrate Preparation

Mix vermiculite and rice flour

Different species of magic mushrooms thrive well on different types of substrate. In wild, they can be found on either dung, grass or wood (chips). Naturally, psilocybe cubensis grows on dung, this could probably explains their lower status in the Mexican teonanácatl cultus. While cultivation at home usually make use of rye or other grains (or a mixture). Pulverized brown rice is used for psilocybe Fantaticus. Mix the grains with vermiculite and water. It is possible to use different ratios.

The recommended substrate for cultivating sclerotia is rice or grass seed.

The basic growkit of 4 small filter boxes works with 220g of rice flour which will be sufficient. Mix in a large bowl the rice flour with 600g vermiculite and 300 ml water and stir until well mixed.

In the lid of each filter box, use a nail or other type of pin to make 4 holes. Fill each of the cultivation boxes with the substrate until it gets to 1 cm from the top of the box. Top it off with about 0.5-0.75 cm layer of vermiculite. The topping off is known as 'casing': which is a method that highly improves the yield by providing some air exchange and also acts as a barrier for contaminants.

Step 2 Sterilizing the substrate

In sterilizing the substrate close the lids, while leaving one side slightly open for pressure to escape and wrap your cultivation boxes in a double layer of aluminium foil. It is preferably when sterilizing the substrate to use a pressure cooker. Although an ordinary cooking pan can work as well (so long as it has a lid that closes well), but this does not guarantee that all bacteria will be killed.

Add the wrapped boxes to the pressure cooker. Make sure the boxes don't touch the pan by putting them in the accompanying basket or you place a towel or cloth at the bottom (this is to prevent cracking). Add enough water to it, and allow it to steam for 60 minutes at 121°C to fully sterilize. If using an ordinary pan increase to 90 minutes. Leave the boxes to cool down completely before proceeding to the next step because a warm substrate will kill the spores. it will take a couple of hours for the boxes to cool down.

Step 3 Inoculation

This is the most riskful part of the process. Ensure that you work in a completely clean and disinfected environment because mycelium are very sensitive to contamination. Do not just disinfect only your workplace but also disinfect all the tools that will be used. Put on a mouth mask and protective gloves.

Thoroughly shake the spore syringe for about 5-10 seconds in order to equally distribute the spores. Take off the safety cap from the needle and place it in a flame till it is red-hot. Allow it cool for about 15-20 seconds. Take off the aluminium foil from the cultivation boxes and inject about 2-3ml of spore suspension on each cultivation box, making use of the four holes you initially prepared. Seal the holes immediately with tape after injecting to prevent contamination.

Step 4 Incubation

Place your cultivation boxes in a dark, warm place. An ideal temperature is 28°C, but room temperature of 20°C is acceptable. When the temperatures is low, it will slow the growth process and temperature below 15°C will inhibits mycelium growth. For the spores to develop fully into mycelium, it requires two to four weeks and the substrate is fully colonised when you notice that all kernels are covered with white mycelium.

When you notice other colours that are not white, it signifies the presence of bacterial or fungal contaminants. When a box is contaminated, it should be discarded immediately. The only exception should be for blue bruising, which is as a results of oxygenation of the psilocybin. Also, small yellow spots are indication of metabolites signifying a slow growth.

Step 5 Mushroom growing

For the mycelium to fruit it is needed that you exposed them to fresh air and light, so now it's time to change the environment. Take out the lids from the cultivation boxes and put them in a filter bag.

The mycelium is less vulnerable to contamination when fully colonized, however it is still important that you work as clean as possible, ensure you wash your hands before opening a filter box or bag.

While growing, the top layer of vermiculite should not be soaking wet but kept moist. Once in a while, make use of a spray bottle to mist the vermiculite layer and inside of the bag. On a general note, when you observe condensation inside of the bag, it means humidity is high enough.

Take the bag to a warm spot of about 20-25°C in the light, but not above a radiator or in the sun. Take daily observation and mist when necessary. When it is 1-2 weeks you will notice the appearance of first pinheads. Within another 1-2 weeks, they grow into mature mushrooms.

MAGIC MUSHROOM

CULTIVATION

The principle of cultivating magic mushroom are generally the same all over the world. The following steps should be carefully followed to achieve the desired results in mushroom cultivation.

Step 1:

Get your grow room ready and ensure that the room is cleaned of dust or other form of dirty could that be found within.

Step 2:

The next step is to set up the Bunsen burner and make sure it's a stable standing, ensure that it is properly set and should not fall on its side!

Step 3:

Get your magic mushrooms spore print, needle and Petri dishes. Ensure you keep the lids on the petri dishes for the time and should only be opened when necessary and closed immediately when done.

Step 4:

Place your magic mushroom spore print ready on the table, hold the front of the needle into the flame of the Bunsen burner and keep it in there until it begins to get a bit red. After which you allow it to cool down. Hold it into the flame again, for about 3 - 5 seconds. Allow it for some few seconds again and ensure that it is not more than room temperature and press it into the spore print, open the Petri dishes and place the needle tip inside the agar-agar and close the Petri dish again. Note that everything has to be done real fast and the Petri dish should not be opened longer than 3 seconds and it is better not to take off the lid completely, you lift it and move it a bit, so that there is just a space of 1 or 2 cm that is exposed directly to the air.

Step 5:

Do this with 3 Petri dishes and put them in a dark room with average temperature. Avoid placing them in direct sunlight because it could be bad and could heat up the Petri dishes in a bad way. Humidity will not be a problem, since the Petri dish is a nice small growing chamber. Between 4-10 days, it will be visible how the magic mushroom started to colonize through the agar-agar.

Step 6:

If your magic mushroom spores already has colonized over the entire Petri dish, they are then set for the next step. Get ready a mix of 1 part rice flour and 1 part Vermiculite and 3 parts organic rye. Spread the mix in the quantity that perfectly fit into your jars. Even when you are sure that it sterile after this step, try also to avoid unnecessary dust, dirt or bad environment like rooms with mold. And before securing the lid, add 2 small coffee cups of water into each of the jar.

Step 7:

Add the preserving jars into your pressure cooker, seal and set it to low heat. Owing to the fact that the preserving jars are made of glass, they could be broken when heated up and cooled down too fast. When the pressure cooker is on full heat, allow it there for 60 minutes. The steam is not as hot as the Bunsen burner, so therefore they needs some more time to make things sterile.

Step 8:

When the jars are sterile, allow them to cool down to room temperature, but you should never make the mistake of opening the lid of the jars, or else you would risk a contamination.

Step 9:

Take your scalpel and the Petri dishes, which are now colonized with your hallucinogenic mushrooms. Sterilize the scalpel on top of the Bunsen burner and allow it cool down, open the lid of the Petri dishes and carefully cut your colonized agar-agar into squares, so that you have around 5-10 of small colonized pieces.

Step 10:

Wear a sterile gloves and if possible use long forceps that are also sterile. Open the lid, get the jars and push in some colonized agar-agar pieces inside them and close it back. Do this in the same manner you did when putting your hallucinogenic mushrooms spores in your Petri dishes.

Step 11:

Keep your jars in a dark room with average temperature like you did with the Petri dishes, after some days, you will notice that the colonization of the magic mushrooms dig through your feeding media. Please note that this step is very essential, when going to the next step, allow it to colonize until half of the jar is filled.

Step 12:

Make ready the same grow media mix which you placed in the jars, and also add the same quantity of water placing them in the pressure cooker. After 15 minutes of full heat, you may take them out and spread it on the ground of the grow boxes. The psychedelic mushrooms are still susceptible to contamination, but they are not as fragile as before.

Step 13:

Remove the colonized material from one jar and mix them under your media prepared in the grow box. Ensure this is done quickly and do not keep the box opened longer than necessary.

Step 14:

Place your box at 24 °C when using the Psilocybe Cubensis specie as your magic mushrooms to grow; inspect it every day to see if the box has a high humidity and if the media is always soaked with water. When you notice that the humidity does not fit, spray them with distilled water. Note that water from the bathroom contains unwanted guest already, watering also depend on the quality of water in your area, which could even cause havoc to a fully colonized box.

Step 15:

After some few days, the magic mushrooms has colonized the media in the entire box and after which they begin to form the parts of the mushrooms you love them for. When they are around half of the flush and has reached a size where the hat is about to open, you can then harvest them.

Step 16:

Lift your magic mushrooms above the ground level and twist them gently, so that they come out almost from themselves and you should not pull with force. Once you finished, spray the box with water again until your media is wet again with water. Your next flush will come within 2 days after which it is ready to be harvested within 1 week.

CHAPTER SEVEN

HARVESTING YOUR MAGIC

MUSHROOM

In most cases it is very difficult to know when you can harvest your mushrooms in your grow kit. Sometimes, it is very much easier if all the mushrooms were the same size and all of them could be harvested at once but this however is never the case. Once your mushrooms are large enough to harvest, there are usually a number of small and medium-sized mushrooms which might still be able to grow a bit more among them. A common mistake most people make is to remove the large mushrooms first, so the medium-sized and small mushrooms can continue to grow. This mistake unknown to many mushroom growers will not increase the harvest and, moreso, you risk contamination of your grow kit.

THE RIGHT TIME TO HARVEST MUSHROOMS

One of the most important question to when growing your magic mushroom is the question of the best time to harvest your mushrooms. The best time to harvest them is when the hats of your magic mushroom have not fully opened and they still have a nice round head. When a mushroom has reached their maximum size, they will begin to open within few days. The round hat will release itself from the stem and acquire a hat-shaped form. When this happens, it shows that the mushrooms wants to reproduce, and will do so by releasing its spores. These spores can be found under de cap of the hat. When this happens, the mushrooms under the hats will become black from the spores released. At this point your mushroom loses its power once the spores are released. Besides, the spores are harmful to the mycelium, and no mushrooms grows.

DRYING AND PRESERVATION OF MUSHROOMS

Haven successfully grown your magic mushroom is only half way the process, there is the need for you to store them appropriately as well in order to maintain their potency. There is nothing that is more exciting than for you to harvest the first flush of your magic mushrooms. It is usually satisfactory to see the fruits of your labour finally pay off and this gives you a much more personal relationship with your magic mushroom.

After harvest, storing your magic mushrooms can sometimes be a very deceitful adventure if you lack the required knowledge of their storage. Magic mushroom are very easy to get damaged, they diminish in their content, and they are prone to decomposition. For these reasons, it is important to know how to safely and securely store.

STORING FRESH MUSHROOMS

Preserving fresh magic mushrooms correctly is fairly straight forward. Magic mushroom can be stored loose in a cool, dark place, such as your fridge, for up to a month. The needed temperature is between 2-4 degrees Celsius. Magic mushrooms can also placed on unbleached kitchen paper. The fridge is an inherently moist place, and too much moisture can cause damage to your mushrooms and by placing magic mushroom on kitchen paper, some of this risk are avoided.

If you choose to store your mushrooms for more than a month, then you may consider to buy a food vacuum packer. When a food vacuum is packed and stored in a fridge, they can last for up to 3 months. Mushrooms however, first need to be properly dried in order to avoid bacterial growth while in the vacuum.

DRYING MUSHROOMS FOR

LONG TERM STORAGE

If you need to storage your magic mushrooms for a very long term, then the magic mushrooms can be dried out and safely stored in a cool, dry and dark place for up to 2-3 years or even longer than that. The only risks to consider are insect infestation, and potential loss of potency owing to the exposure to light, moisture and heat. This works perfectly because without their moisture content, magic mushrooms pretty much stop decomposing.

The idea of drying magic mushrooms for storage is not to use any heat. This is a common mistake most people make, and often used it to try to speed up the drying process. The active compounds of your magic mushrooms can be quite sensitive to prolonged periods of heat, damaging them or their reducing potency.

The means of drying your magic mushroom harvest first has to do with pre-drying them to remove any excess moisture, closely followed by a thorough main dry using a desiccant. This process will help remove all available moisture leaving your mushrooms ready to be moved into long term storage.

NOTE: Never freeze fresh magic mushrooms, freezing them will destroy their internal cell membrane structure, greatly diminishing potency.

Now you know how to properly and effectively store your magic mushrooms, making sure that their integrity is maintained and that they are set for use whenever you need them.